MW01038281

OCEANS ALIVE

Squids

by Colleen Sexton

BELLWETHER MEDIA • MINNEAPOLIS, MN

Note to Librarians, Teachers, and Parents:

Blastoff! Readers are carefully developed by literacy experts and combine standards-based content with developmentally appropriate text.

Level 1 provides the most support through repetition of high-frequency words, light text, predictable sentence patterns, and strong visual support.

Level 2 offers early readers a bit more challenge through varied simple sentences, increased text load, and less repetition of high-frequency words.

Level 3 advances early-fluent readers toward fluency through increased text and concept load, less reliance on visuals, longer sentences, and more literary language.

Level 4 builds reading stamina by providing more text per page, increased use of punctuation, greater variation in sentence patterns, and increasingly challenging vocabulary.

Level 5 encourages children to move from "learning to read" to "reading to learn" by providing even more text, varied writing styles, and less familiar topics.

Whichever book is right for your reader, Blastoff! Readers are the perfect books to build confidence and encourage a love of reading that will last a lifetime!

This edition first published in 2008 by Bellwether Media.

No part of this publication may be reproduced in whole or in part without written permission of the publisher. For information regarding permission, write to Bellwether Media Inc., Attention: Permissions Department, Post Office Box 19349, Minneapolis, MN 55419.

Library of Congress Cataloging-in-Publication Data
Sexton, Colleen A., 1967–
 Squids / by Colleen Sexton.
   p. cm. – (Blastoff! readers: Oceans alive)
Summary: "Simple text and full color photographs introduce beginning readers to squids. Developed by literacy experts for students in kindergarten through third grade"–Provided by publisher.
 Includes bibliographical references and index.
 ISBN-13: 978-1-60014-175-1 (hardcover : alk. paper)
 ISBN-10: 1-60014-175-7 (hardcover : alk. paper)
 1. Squids–Juvenile literature. I. Title.

QL430.2.S49 2008
594'.58–dc22   2007040280

Contents

Squids are animals that live in the ocean. They swim in both deep and **shallow** waters.

4

Some squids swim alone.
Other squids swim in
large groups.

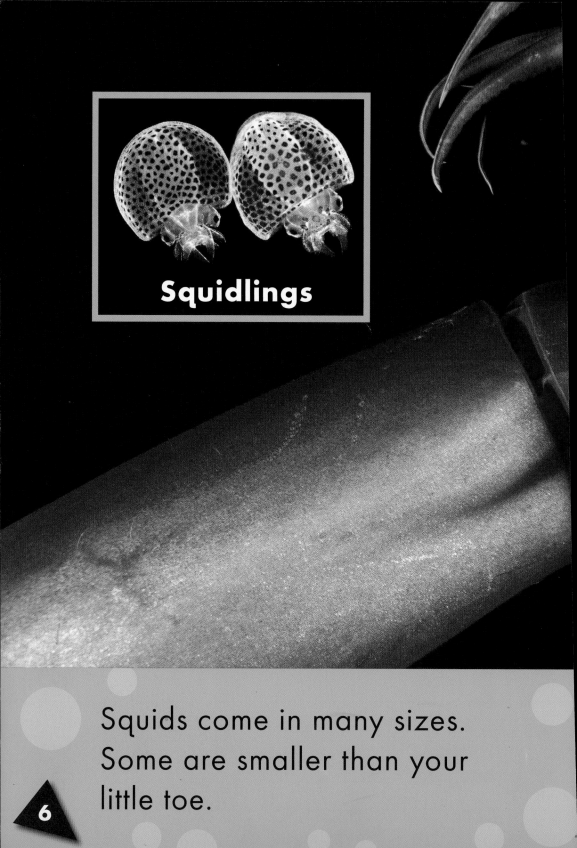

Squidlings

Squids come in many sizes.
Some are smaller than your
little toe.

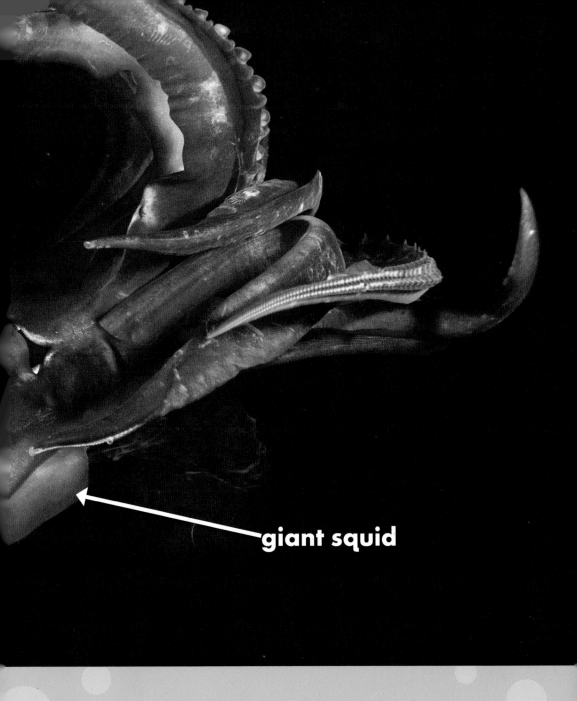

giant squid

A kind of squid called a giant squid can grow as long as two buses.

fins

Squids have a soft body with two **fins** at the end. They breathe through **gills**.

8

Squids have two huge eyes.
Large eyes help squids see
in dark places.

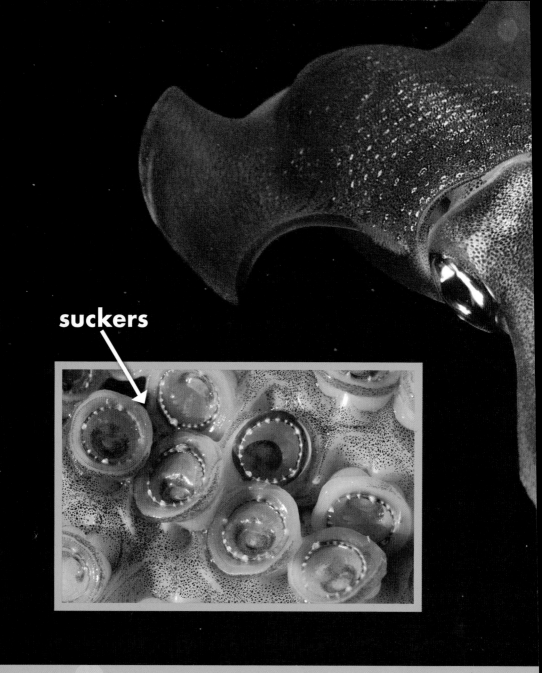

suckers

Most squids have two long **tentacles**. The tentacles have **suckers** at the ends.

10

tentacles

Squids snap their tentacles
forward to catch fish and
other **prey**.

Squids use their tentacles to move food into their mouth.

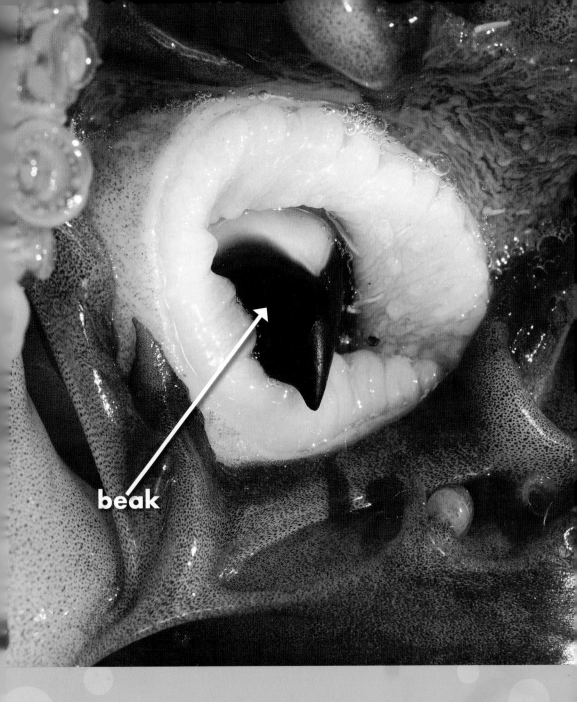

beak

Squids have a hard **beak** for a mouth. They use the beak to tear food.

13

Squids have eight short arms.
Each arm has suckers for
holding onto food.

14

Squids can also feel, smell, and taste with their suckers.

Squids have a **funnel**. This long, hollow muscle inside squids helps them swim.

Squids bring water into the funnel. They push a jet of the water out to move forward.

Squids can swim fast to escape whales, sharks, and other **predators**.

Squids can also hide from predators. They change colors to match their **surroundings**.

19

Squids can make it hard for predators to see. They squirt clouds of **ink** into the water.

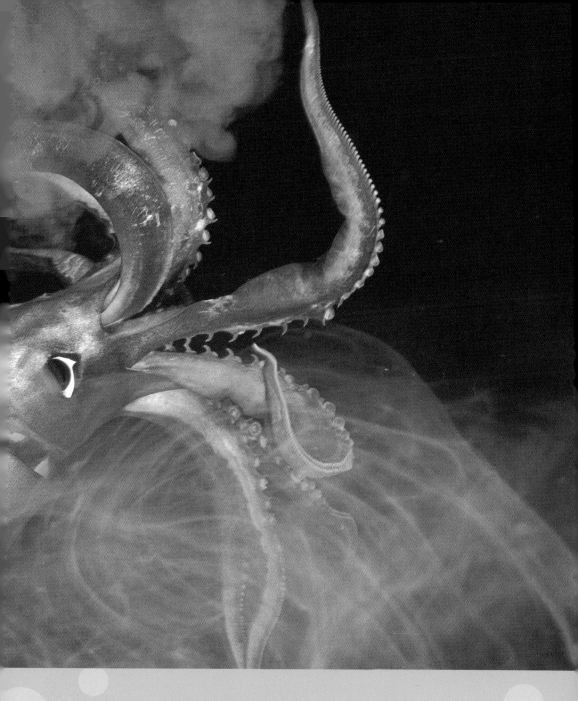

Then squids can escape. They swim away from the ink and leave the predator behind.

21

Glossary

beak—the hard part of the mouth in some animals such as birds, turtles, and squids

fins—flaps on a squid's body used for stopping and steering in the water

funnel—a strong muscle shaped like a tube in a squid's body; squids bring water into the funnel and then push it out to move forward.

gills—openings on a squid that it uses to breathe; gills move oxygen from the water to the squid's blood.

ink—a liquid that squids can squirt from their bodies

predator—an animal that hunts other animals for food; whales, sharks, and sea turtles are some of the predators that eat squids.

prey—an animal hunted by another animal for food

shallow—not deep

suckers—round, cup-shaped parts on a squid's arms and tentacles; suckers can bend and stretch to hold onto things.

surroundings—the area around something; a squid can change its color to match the rocks and plants around it.

tentacles—long, thin arms used for catching food

To Learn More

AT THE LIBRARY
Rake, Jody Sullivan. *Squids*. Mankato, Minn.: Pebble Books, 2007.

Redmond, Shirley-Raye. *Tentacles! Tales of the Giant Squid*. New York: Random House, 2003.

Weber, Valerie J. *Squids*. Milwaukee, Wisc.: Gareth Stevens, 2005.

ON THE WEB
Learning more about squids is as easy as 1, 2, 3.

1. Go to www.factsurfer.com

2. Enter "squids" into search box.

3. Click the "Surf" button and you will see a list of related web sites.

With factsurfer.com, finding more information is just a click away.

Index

The images in this book are reproduced through the courtesy of: Inga Ivanova, front cover; Fred Bavendam/Getty Images, pp. 4-5; Peter Parks/imagequestmarine.com, p. 6 (inset); Brian J. Skerry/Getty Images, pp. 6-7; David Fleetham/Alamy, pp. 8-9; Mark Conlin/V&W/Image Quest Marine, p. 10 (inset); Reinhard Dirscherl /Alamy, pp. 10-11; Roger Steene/imagequest3d. com, p. 12; Mark Conlin/V&W/Image Quest Marine, p. 13; Mark Conlin/V&W/Image Quest Marine, pp. 14-15; James D. Watt/imagequest3d.com, pp. 16-17; Chris Newbert/Getty Images, pp. 18-19; Stephen Frink/Getty Images, p. 17; Konrad Wothe/Getty Images, pp. 18-19; Brian J. Skerry/Getty Images, pp. 20-21.